D0305961

Plan Prepare Cook

A Tasty Breakfast

Rita Storey

W

FRANKLIN WATTS

LONDON•SYDNEY

Contents

First published in 2011 by
Franklin Watts
338 Euston Road
London NW1 3BH

Franklin Watts Australia
Level 17/207 Kent Street
Sydney NSW 2000

© Franklin Watts 2011
Series editor: Sarah Peutrill
Art director: Jonathan Hair

Series designed and created for Franklin Watts by
Storeybooks
Designer: Rita Storey
Editor: Nicola Barber
Photography: Tudor Photography

A CIP catalogue record for this book is available
from the British Library
Printed in China

Dewey classification: 641.5'2

ISBN 978 1 4451 0108 8

Picture credits
All photographs Tudor Photography, Banbury
unless otherwise stated. Shutterstock p5;
Wishlistimages.co.uk p4

Cover images Tudor Photography
All photos posed by models. Thanks to Serena
Clayton, Adam Hedley and Emma Whitehouse.

Franklin Watts is a division of Hachette Children's
Books, an Hachette UK company
www.hachette.co.uk

Pages marked with ⬇ have a related downloadable free activity sheet at www.franklinwatts/downloads. Find out more on page 32.

Words in **bold** are in the glossary on page 30.

Before you start

These simple rules will make sure you stay safe when you cook:

- Wash your hands before and after preparing food.
- Ask an adult to help when the recipe uses the cooker or grill.
- If you have long hair, clip or tie it back.
- Dry your hands before you plug in or unplug any electrical appliances.
- Wear an apron or an old shirt.
- Wash up as you go along.
- Be extra careful with sharp knives.
- Ask an adult to help with the liquidiser/food processor.
- Ask an adult to help you weigh the ingredients.

Look out for this useful guide to each recipe.

How long each recipe takes to make.

How difficult each recipe is to make.

If the recipe needs to be cooked.

All about breakfast

What you eat and drink is called your **diet**. To eat a **balanced diet** try not to have the same foods every day. There are so many lovely foods and drinks to choose from at breakfast time – why stick to the same things every day?

The human machine

The human body is a machine that needs **energy** to work. Energy is released from the food we eat and used by our bodies.

Meat, fish, chicken, eggs and beans

These foods contain **protein**. Eggs are often eaten at breakfast time.

Fruit and vegetables

You should eat at least five portions of fruit and vegetables every day. They should make up about a third of what you eat. Frozen, canned and dried fruits and vegetables all count. Try to eat lots of different types.

• A glass of fruit juice counts as one portion, so try to have one at breakfast time.

Make a good start

Eating a good breakfast will give you the energy to concentrate throughout the morning. If you do not have breakfast you may feel tired and grumpy until you can eat at lunchtime.

Exercise

When you **exercise** you use up the energy from the food you have eaten.

To be healthy you need to eat enough food but not too much. If you eat more food than your body needs, it is turned into **fat**. If you do this all the time, you keep getting fatter.

Playing a sport, walking, riding your bike or dancing are all good ways to exercise.

Other people may enjoy exercising with you!

Starchy foods

You should eat **starchy** foods every day – they should make up about a third of what you eat. A portion of bread or cereal at breakfast time is a good start to the day.

• Choose **wholegrain** or **wholewheat** varieties.

A healthy body

To stay healthy your body needs some things found in food and drink. **Vitamins** and **minerals** help to stop you getting ill. You also need them for your body to grow and work properly. Different foods contain different vitamins and minerals. To make sure you get all the vitamins and minerals you need, eat plenty of fruit and vegetables as well as a range of other foods. **Fibre** is needed to help your body **digest** the food you eat.

Milk and yoghurt

Milk and all types of yoghurt are a good choice on cereals at breakfast time.

• Use **semi-skimmed** milk as it has less fat.

• Look at the labels on yoghurts and choose the ones lowest in sugar and fat.

Shopping and planning

Planning, preparing and cooking great-tasting food for yourself, friends and family, is great fun and you get to eat well too!

Think of all the things you would like to make for breakfast in the next week. Look through this book for some new ideas for breakfast recipes. Make a shopping list of the things you need.

Make a shopping list of the things you need to make a tasty breakfast every day for a week.

Go shopping

If you go shopping for food, look at the food labels. Some foods are very good for you. Foods that are high in salt, sugar or fat are bad for you if you eat them too often.

• Choose wholegrain or wholewheat bread and breakfast cereals. They have lots of vitamins, minerals and fibre (see page 5). They also have lots of flavour.

• Look for low-salt, low-sugar and low-fat foods (particularly if the fat is **saturated fat**) on food labels.

Plan ahead

Breakfast time can be a rush, so prepare things in advance if you can. Pancake **batter**, fruit salad and smoothie drinks can all be made the night before you need them and kept in the fridge. Fruit bars (see pages 16-17) will keep for a few days in a plastic container.

When you wake up you will know that you can make a delicious breakfast in double-quick time.

Water

You need water for your body to perform well. You get some water from the foods you eat. You should drink six to eight glasses of water a day – more in hot weather.

Sugar, fat and processed foods

Foods from this group should only be eaten occasionally.
• Avoid white bread and white sugar.
• Look for cereals that do not have added sugar.
• Sausages and bacon are often eaten for breakfast. They have a lot of fat in them. Just have them every now and again as a treat.
• Use only a small amount of butter or oil in cooking.

Make sure you drink enough water.

Fruit smoothie

Not all healthy breakfasts are cooked. This simple fruit smoothie drink has lots of good things in it to give you energy in the morning.

You will need

- measuring jug
- liquidiser (or food processor)
- dessertspoon
- drinking glass
- drinking straw

Ingredients

- 1 ripe banana
- some strawberries or raspberries
- 425 ml (15 fl oz) milk
- 5 dessertspoons Greek yoghurt

This will make enough for two large glasses.

If you prefer

Use banana or strawberry yoghurt instead of Greek yoghurt.

Add a teaspoon of honey to unsweetened yoghurt.

1

- Peel the banana.
- Put the banana and any other fruits you are using in the liquidiser.

2

- Measure 425 ml (15 fl oz) of milk in the measuring jug.
- Pour the milk into the liquidiser.

- Put 5 dessertspoons of Greek yoghurt in the liquidiser.

4

- Put the lid on the liquidiser. Turn the liquidiser on.

5

- Whizz everything together until there are no lumps.

6

- Pour the mixture into a glass and enjoy a healthy and delicious breakfast drink.

Mmm!

Handy hint

This drink will keep for two days in a screw-top bottle in the fridge.

10 minutes

Very easy

No cooking

Fruit salad

This colourful fruit salad is a fresh and tasty way to start the day.

Ingredients

- selection of different coloured fruits: satsumas, bananas, strawberries, kiwi fruit, blueberries, seedless grapes (about 90 g (3 oz) per person)
- teaspoon of lemon juice
- 125 ml (4 fl oz) unsweetened fruit juice

You will need

- kitchen paper
- sharp knife
- cutting board
- teaspoon
- peeler
- mixing bowl
- mixing spoon
- bowl and spoon

Handy hint

Different coloured fruits and vegetables contain a variety of vitamins and minerals (see page 5).

Before you start

- Wash the fruit and pat it dry on kitchen paper.

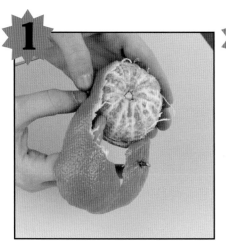

1

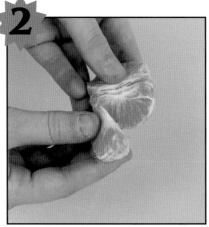

2

Satsumas
- Take off the peel.

- Divide into segments.

Bananas
- Peel and slice. Toss in the lemon juice to stop the slices going brown.

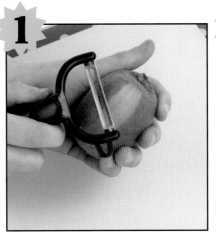

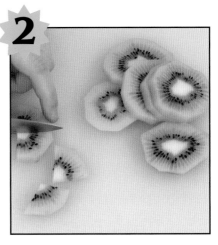

Strawberries
- Take off the leaves and stems. Cut in half.

Kiwi fruit
- Using the peeler, take off the peel.

- Cut into slices. Cut the slices into half, and then in half again.

- Put the prepared fruit into the mixing bowl with the unsweetened fruit juice. Mix together.

Grapes
Cut in half.

Beautiful!

Serve in a plain bowl to show up all the lovely rainbow colours.

15 minutes

Medium

No cooking

Berry cereal

A bowl of cereal is a quick and easy breakfast. To make it into a really healthy meal, add a handful of fresh berries.

You will need

- sieve
- kitchen paper
- cutting board
- small sharp knife
- cereal bowl
- spoon

Ingredients

- handful of berries such as strawberries, raspberries, blackberries or blueberries
- portion of cereal
- semi-skimmed milk

Choosing a breakfast cereal
Look at the ingredients list on the packet of breakfast cereal. If possible, use a breakfast cereal that does not have any added sugar. The best kind of cereal is wholegrain or wholewheat with nothing else added. If necessary you can sweeten it yourself with a small amount of sugar or honey.

1

- Put the berries in the sieve and rinse in cold water.

2

- Pat them dry with a piece of kitchen paper.

3

- Cut large fruits into smaller pieces.

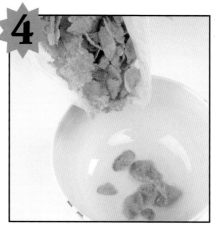

4

- Measure the cereal into a bowl.

5

- Pour on the milk.

6

- Sprinkle on the berries.

Handy hint

You can use other fruits if you prefer. See pages 10 and 11 for how to prepare them.

Wow!

5 minutes

Very easy

No cooking

Yoghurt mix-up

This messy, crunchy breakfast is full of healthy things to get your day off to a good start. Try making it with your favourite breakfast cereal.

Ingredients

- 1 small banana
- 3 dessertspoons Greek yoghurt
- a heaped tablespoon of branflakes or cornflakes
- honey

You will need

- kitchen knife
- mixing bowl
- mixing spoon
- cereal bowl
- spoon

If you prefer

You can use any type of yoghurt or **fromage frais** in this recipe. Try a few different combinations. Other fruits such as chunks of apple and apricots are also very good. Only use honey if the yoghurt is unsweetened.

Yoghurt

Yoghurt contains **calcium** which helps to build strong bones and teeth. It also contains protein, vitamins and minerals. Low-fat yoghurt contains all these things but has less fat. Some yoghurt has a lot of sugar added to it.

1

- Peel the banana.
- Slice it and put the slices in the mixing bowl.

- Put the yoghurt into the mixing bowl.

- Add the cereal.
- Mix everything together gently so that the flakes of cereal do not get too broken up.

- Serve in a cereal bowl with a drizzle of honey.

Yummmmm

5 minutes

Very easy

No cooking

Whizzy fruit bar

If there really is no time for breakfast, try one of these bars instead. They are packed full of fruity energy.

You will need

- food processor (or liquidiser)
- small saucepan
- wooden spoon
- baking tray
- knife
- small sieve

Ingredients

- 115 g (4 oz) trail mix (a mixture of dried fruits and nuts)
- 30 g (1 oz) mini marshmallows
- 1 tablespoon of water
- 1 teaspoon icing sugar

Handy hint

Sugar is bad for your teeth. If you have any foods that contain sugar at breakfast time remember to brush your teeth afterwards.

1
- Tip the trail mix into the food processor.

2
- Whizz it up until there are no big lumps.

3
- Put the marshmallows and water into a small saucepan. Put the pan on the hob on a low heat.

- Stir with the wooden spoon until the marshmallows have melted.

- Add the whizzed trail mix and stir until well mixed.

- Tip the mixture into the baking tray.
* Remember to turn the hob off.

- Press the mixture down with the knife. Put in the fridge.
- When set, cut into squares.

- Sieve the icing sugar over the fruit bars.

Scrummy!

| 1 hour |
| Easy |
| Cooked |

Cheesy eggs

Eggs are a good, healthy breakfast choice. There are lots of different ways to cook them for breakfast.

Ingredients

- 2 eggs
- 1 dessertspoon grated cheese (see page 29)
- 1 slice wholemeal bread, muffin or bagel toasted
- 30 g (1 oz) butter

You will need

- small mixing bowl
- fork
- dessertspoon
- knife
- small non-stick saucepan
- wooden spoon
- plate

Bread

Bread is made from wheat. It is a starchy food, like pasta, potatoes and rice. Bread has vitamins, minerals and fibre in it (see page 5). Most types of white bread have less fibre than wholemeal bread.

1

- Crack the eggs into the mixing bowl (see page 28).
- Whisk the eggs with the fork until the white and the yolk are all mixed together.

2

- Stir in the grated cheese with a spoon.

3

- Spread the bagel with half the butter.
- Turn on the hob. Put the pan on the hob on a low heat.

- Melt the other half of the butter in the saucepan on the hob.

- Pour the egg and cheese mixture into the saucepan.

- Stir the mixture with the wooden spoon until it is cooked. You will see the colour of the mixture change as you stir it.
* Remember to turn the hob off.

- Put the buttered bagel on the plate. Spoon the cheesy eggs on to it. Add a sprinkle of grated cheese.

Cheesylicious!

| 10 minutes |
| Medium |
| Cooked |

'Just right' porridge

The three bears in the 'Goldilocks' story knew all about eating a good breakfast. A bowl of porridge is a great way to start the day. Oats are cheap to buy and easy to cook.

Ingredients

- 60 g (2 oz) porridge oats
- 300 ml (10 fl oz) semi-skimmed milk
- handful of cranberries
- drizzle of maple syrup or golden syrup

Oats

Oats are a starchy food (see page 5). They are used up slowly in your body so they make you feel full for a long time. They also contain lots of fibre. Buy 'rolled oats' or 'porridge oats' rather than 'instant oats'. Oats should be the only ingredient in the packet!

You will need

- measuring jug
- small non-stick saucepan
- wooden spoon
- cereal bowl and spoon

1

2

- Put the oats into the saucepan and add the milk.
- Turn the hob on to a medium heat.

- Stir the porridge with the wooden spoon.
- When the porridge starts to bubble, turn the heat down to low and keep stirring for 2 minutes.
- * Remember to turn the hob off.

- Spoon the porridge mixture into a cereal bowl.
- Top with the cranberries.

- Add a drizzle of maple syrup or golden syrup.

Scrumptious

Handy hint
When you have put the cooked porridge into the bowl, fill the dirty saucepan with water to make it easier to wash up.

5 minutes

Easy

Cooked

Muesli magic

Muesli is a breakfast cereal made from rolled oats mixed with nuts, seeds and dried fruits. You can eat it with milk or use this recipe to turn it into something really special to impress your family and friends.

You will need

- 2 mixing bowls
- 2 mixing spoons
- tall glass
- tablespoon

Ingredients

- 30 g (1 oz) rolled oats
- 30 g (1 oz) dried fruits (sultanas, apricots, dried apple chunks, cranberries) and 30 g (1 oz) chopped nuts
- 2 tablespoons plain thick, Greek or vanilla yoghurt
- 1 tablespoon of fruit **coulis**
- 60 g (2 oz) raspberries
- honey

Muesli
You can buy muesli ready-mixed in a packet. Look on the packet for a muesli that has no added sugar and salt. Many prepared cereals contain a lot of sugar and salt.

1

- Mix the oats, fruits and nuts in a bowl.

2

- In another bowl mix the fruit coulis with 1 tablespoon of yoghurt.

- Put 1 tablespoon of plain yoghurt in the bottom of the glass.
- Sprinkle a layer of muesli on top of the yoghurt.
- Add a layer of raspberries.

- Add a layer of the yoghurt and fruit coulis mixture.
- Finish with a layer of muesli and a drizzle of honey.

Mmmmm

10 minutes

Easy

No cooking

23

Fruit pancake

Pancakes are made from a mixture of milk, flour and eggs, called batter. Make a stack and fill with your favourite fruits.

You will need

- sieve
- mixing bowl
- teaspoon
- tablespoon
- fork
- measuring jug
- whisk
- frying pan
- fish slice
- plate

Ingredients

- 115 g (4 oz) plain flour
- 2 teaspoons baking powder
- pinch of salt
- 1 tablespoon sugar
- 1 egg
- 175 ml (6 fl oz) milk
- 1 tablespoon oil
- a few tablespoons of prepared fruit
- creme fraiche
- chopped nuts
- golden syrup

This will make 12 pancakes.

Other fillings

- apple sauce and a sprinkle of cinnamon
- cherry pie filling and a spoonful of ice cream

1

2

3

- Sieve the flour, baking powder and salt into the mixing bowl.
- Add the sugar.

- Crack the egg into the jug (see page 28). Whisk it up with a fork.

- Add the egg to the dry ingredients in the mixing bowl.
- Add the milk.

24

4

- Whisk it all together.
- Put half a teaspoon of oil into a frying pan. Heat the frying pan over a medium heat.

5

- Drop in a tablespoon of batter.
- Cook for about a minute until bubbles appear on the surface.

6

- Turn the pancake over with the fish slice. Cook the other side for about a minute.

7

- Place the pancake on a plate and keep warm.
- Make more pancakes until all the mixture is used.
- Stack the pancakes, putting fruit and creme fraiche between them.
- Top with chopped nuts and golden syrup.
- * Remember to turn the hob off when the cooking is finished.

Perfect

30 minutes

Tricky!

Cooked

Eggs and toast

The combination of boiled egg and crunchy wholewheat toast fingers make a perfect breakfast. The egg and toast are easy to cook and good for you too.

Ingredients

- 1 egg
- 1 slice wholemeal bread, toasted
- 30 g (1 oz) butter

You will need

- small saucepan
- egg timer
- tablespoon
- egg cup
- small plate
- teaspoon
- knife

Eggs

Eggs are a good source of protein, and contain vitamins and minerals.

Free range eggs are from hens that are allowed to run around in the open air.

Barn eggs are from hens that are kept in big barns.

Battery eggs are from birds that are kept in cages.

1

- Turn the hob on high.
- Put the egg into the saucepan and cover it with cold water.
Put it on the hob.

2

- When the water starts to **boil** (see page 29) turn the egg timer over.
If you do not have an egg timer, time three minutes on a clock.
- When all the sand has gone to the bottom of the timer, lift the egg out of the pan with the tablespoon.

- Put the egg into the egg cup.
* Remember to turn the hob off.
- Cut the top off the egg with the spoon, or peel off the egg shell. Be careful it will be hot.

- Butter the toast.

- Cut it into strips.

- Dip the strips into the egg.

Lovely

| 10 minutes |
| Easy |
| Cooked |

How to!

Crack open an egg

- Tap the egg gently on the side of a bowl so that it cracks.

- Put your thumbs on either side of the crack.

- Hold the egg over the bowl and gently pull the shell apart.

Use a sieve

You can sieve flour and icing sugar to get rid of any lumps.

- Place the sieve on top of a bowl.
- Put the measured ingredient (usually flour or icing sugar) into the sieve.
- Lift the sieve up above the bowl and gently tap it against the palm of your hand. The sieved flour or sugar will fall into the bowl. Any lumps of flour or sugar can be gently pushed through the sieve with a spoon.

Grate

1

- Hold the top of the grater to stop it slipping.

2

- Press food against the blades and push down.

- A food grater has lots of sharp blades that can turn food into strips.
- A box grater has different-sized blades for different foods.
- Cheese and carrots are best grated on the largest blades.
- The smallest blades are for grating the rind off oranges and lemons.

Whisk

To whisk means to stir something quickly to mix everything together. Whisking adds air to a mixture to make it lighter.

- A whisk is a kitchen utensil designed for whisking liquids.

- This egg is being whisked with a fork.

Know when water is boiling

- Cold water does not have any bubbles.
- As the water heats up, small bubbles rise to the surface. The water is **simmering**.

- As the water gets hotter the bubbles get larger and pop as they rise to the surface. The water is now boiling.

Glossary

balanced diet A diet that contains all the foods necessary to grow and stay healthy.

batter A mixture of flour, egg and milk, used for making pancakes and Yorkshire puddings, or to coat food before it is fried.

boiling The point at which water (or another liquid) reaches a heat when it bubbles and turns into steam.

calcium A mineral that the body needs to develop healthy bones and teeth. Calcium is found in foods such as milk, yoghurt and cheese.

coulis A thick sauce made from fruit.

diet The things that you eat and drink.

digest To break down food inside the body so that it can be converted into energy.

energy A type of power that can be used. Food is changed to energy in your body.

exercise Physical activity that uses up calories and improves fitness.

fat A greasy substance found in food. Fats are divided into two types: **saturated fats** are found in cream, cheese, butter, suet, lard, fatty meat and chocolate; **unsaturated fats** are found in avocados, nuts, vegetable oils and olive oils. Unsaturated fats are healthier than saturated fats.

fibre The part of a fruit or vegetable that cannot be digested. Fibre helps the digestion of other food.

fromage frais A type of low-fat, soft cheese that tastes similar to natural yoghurt. It can be used in both sweet and savoury recipes.

mineral A substance such as iron and calcium that the body needs to function properly. Minerals are found in foods.

processed food Any food product that has been changed in some way. Cooking, freezing, drying, canning and preserving are all methods of processing food. Processed foods may contain colourings, flavourings and other additives and preservatives.

protein A substance found in some foods. It is needed by the body to grow and develop properly. Meat, eggs, milk and some types of bean contain protein.

semi-skimmed A type of milk that has had half of the cream removed.

simmering To bring a liquid almost to a boil. A simmering liquid has small bubbles that rise to the surface.

starchy A food containing starch. Starchy foods make up one of the food groups. They include bread, cereals, rice, pasta and potatoes.

vitamin One of the substances that are essential in very small amounts in the body for normal growth and activity.

wholegrain A cereal such as wheat, barley or oats that have not had the outer layer taken off.

wholewheat The entire grain of wheat including the outer layer (bran).

Equipment

little sieve/tea strainer

big sieve

cutting board

measuring jug

fish slice

mixing bowl

grater

mixing spoon

whisk

tablespoon

dessertspoon

teaspoon

non-stick saucepan

knife

small sharp knife

frying pan

egg timer

wooden spoons

You will also need:
T-towel
weighing scales
oven glove

kitchen paper

liquidiser

food processor

Index

Activity sheets

The following pages have accompanying sheets, which are available to download for free at www.franklinwatts.co.uk.

Pages 4–5 All about breakfast
Plan your breakfasts for the week ahead on this handy food chart. Fill in the shopping list so you know what you need to buy.

Pages 6–7 All about breakfast
What do your friends eat for breakfast? Fill in this food survey to find out what is the most popular breakfast.

Page 31 Equipment
Download a colourful poster of all the equipment used in the 'Plan Prepare Cook' books.